100

THINGS TO DO IN
NYC
NEW YORK CITY
BEFORE YOU
DIE

100

THINGS TO DO IN
NYC
NEW YORK CITY
BEFORE YOU
DIE

• •

JAMES HEIDENRY

REEDY PRESS
St. Louis, Missouri

To Lauren, Zac and Riley,
who are always at the top of my list

Reedy Press
PO Box 5131
St. Louis, MO 63139, USA
www.reedypress.com

Library of Congress Control Number: 2014905725

ISBN: 978-1-935806-73-8

Design by Jill Halpin

Printed in the United States of America
14 15 16 17 18   5 4 3 2 1

Please note that websites, phone numbers, addresses, and company names are subject to change or cancellation. We did our best to relay the most accurate information available, but due to circumstances beyond our control, please do not hold us liable for misinformation. When exploring new destinations, please do your homework before you go.

CONTENTS

• •

• •

PREFACE

Dear Passing Stranger!

New York is a big city. And as you may have heard, it never sleeps, if you can make it here you can make it anywhere, and it's a concrete jungle where dreams are made. More than 8 million people from all over the world call the Big Apple home, and another 50 million or so visit it every year. And for good reason. Because no matter what your interests—food, architecture, shopping, sightseeing, theater, music, art, romance, adventure—New York is where it's at.

One of the open secrets to this city's vitality is the ease with which a person can travel from the Lower East Side to Midtown, from Brooklyn to SoHo, from Grand Central Station to Yankee Stadium. Unlike other mega metropolises in the U.S. and around the globe, New York is a city where you can take a subway, bus, or taxi to wherever you want to go, whenever you want to go there. Public transportation runs around the clock, and taxi drivers will risk death to get you to your destination as quickly as traffic lights and traffic allow. And yet, at the heart of NYC is Manhattan, an island best discovered on foot.

• •

I was born at the top of Manhattan in Inwood, and now reside at the bottom, in the West Village, with my wife and two children. For many years in between those two locations I traveled and lived abroad, constantly visiting worthy tourist traps and searching out little-known experiences with equal resolve and enthusiasm. The raison d'être for *100 Things to Do in New York Before You Die* is to help residents and tourists alike understand—and become a part of—the wondrous allure of this great, spinning city.

Each of these "100 Things" is a one-of-a-kind experience, guaranteed to provide a memory that you will longingly revisit many times over. Of course, New York should really be enjoyed on an individual's own, private terms. So take a seat on a park bench or the steps of the Metropolitan Museum of Art and watch the world go by, venture down one of those oddball streets in the garment district and walk into an oddball shop, or plot a stroll through an unfamiliar neighborhood and you'll discover a city that no book can capture. With ears, eyes, and mind open, you'll find all the things that make New York so special, whatever they may be.

—James Heidenry

100

THINGS TO DO IN
NYC
NEW YORK CITY
BEFORE YOU
DIE

CRUISE PAST
THE STATUE OF LIBERTY

All those poor, tired, huddled masses would have headed straight back to the Old Country if they had faced the lines that typically greet patriots and tourists looking to visit Liberty Island. The best way to see America's First Lady is to take the Circle Line cruise, which departs from Pier 83, down the Hudson River. It passes close by Lady Liberty before heading under the Brooklyn and Manhattan bridges. (There are many Circle Line cruise options, so make sure you choose the right one. A good alternative is to ride the Staten Island Ferry, which gets pretty close to the Great Lady, runs regularly, and is free!)

Pier 83: W. 42nd St., 212-563-3200, circleline42.com

HIT MoMA'S
GARDEN PARTY

One of New York's most famous museums is the Museum of Modern Art, which was founded by members of the Rockefeller family and remains one of its pet projects to this day. A daylong visit is a must because of the enormous collection of Picassos, Pollocks, and de Koonings as well as an endless rotation of extraordinary special exhibitions. MoMA is equally well known for its garden party, an annual event to fête big-bucks trustees who have their names chiseled into the museum's marble walls. The rabble is understandably barred from the sit-down dinner inside, but for $200 you can party in the Sculpture Garden, where all the fun is to be had anyway. Best of all, of-the-moment acts like Kanye West and Fun are always booked for entertainment, and the good times last till midnight!

11 W. 53rd St., 212-708-9400, moma.org

ATTEND
THE U.S. OPEN

Unlike seeing the Yankees, Mets, Knicks, Nets, Jets, Giants, Rangers, or Islanders in action, a trip to the U.S. Open never disappoints . . . unless it rains. For starters, the world-class facilities at the USTA Billie Jean King National Tennis Center, located in Queens, are easily accessible. It boasts 32 courts in addition to the 22,547-seat Arthur Ashe Stadium, which is named after the famous African-American tennis player who won the U.S. Open in 1968—the first year professionals were allowed to compete. It's the largest tennis venue in the world and has been the scene of some of the sport's most epic battles: Pete Sampras besting Andre Agassi in the 2001 quarterfinal (neither player ever broke the other's serve), Venus Williams defeating her sister Serena in the 2001 Grand Slam final, and Novak Kjokovic upsetting Roger Federer in the 2010 semifinal. But you don't need to see the gods of tennis play to have a good time—qualifying matches are a great option. The tickets are cheaper and easier to get, and the level of play is still mind-blowing.

usopen.org

EXPLORE
THE NORTHWEST AREA
OF CENTRAL PARK

Ask any New Yorker for a short list of must-sees in Central Park and they'll likely rattle off destinations like Strawberry Fields and Bethesda Fountain. But if you ask Central Park's historian, Sara Cedar Millar, for her favorite spot, she'll probably send you up north to the now-defunct bridle paths. This area has a distinct topography (complete with waterfall), making it a favorite among naturalists and joggers alike.

212-310-6600, centralparknyc.org

HAVE A DRINK
AT MARRIOTT MARQUIS
IN TIMES SQUARE

Make no mistake about it—Times Square is one of the worst places on earth, right behind Guantanamo Bay prison and wherever they film *Cops*. Yet, at night, all those Jumbotrons and neon lights are undeniably mesmerizing. Head to the Broadway Lounge bar at the top of the Marriott (take a moment to appreciate the hotel's "sky lobby"), order a cocktail, and look out the window. You now have a new reality.

1535 Broadway, 212-398-1900, marriott.com

LISTEN TO LIVE JAZZ
IN GREENWICH VILLAGE

What? You think John Coltrane is really dead? There are three known cures for jazz know-nothings in NYC: Smalls, the Village Vanguard, and the Blue Note. The latter two venues have been around for the better part of a century, but all three attract the very best talent and have atmospheres that make for one of those late nights to remember. Go alone or with a pal, and hear firsthand the city's one true soundtrack.

Smalls: 183 W. 10th St., 212-252-5091, smallsjazzclub.com
Village Vanguard: 178 7th Ave., 212-255-4037, villagevanguard.com
Blue Note: 131 W. 3rd St., 212-475-8592, bluenotejazz.com

SHOP
AT BERGDORF GOODMAN

At the corner of 58th Street and Fifth Avenue, where a Vanderbilt mansion once stood, is the city's temple to high fashion and conspicuous consumption. Founded in 1899 by Herman Bergdorf, the department store carries all the usual—Prada, Chanel—but it is also known for identifying and selling the best from upstart designers from around the world. Splurge on something, even if it's only a glass of wine in Goodman's Cafe.

754 Fifth Ave., 212-753-7300, bergdorfgoodman.com

WALK ACROSS
THE BROOKLYN BRIDGE

Back in 1870, many a young engineer was trying to figure out how to build a suspension bridge from Brooklyn to Manhattan, but only one had the capability to do it—John Augustus Roebling. Sure, an estimated 27 men died building it, but such was the cost of getting from point A to point B when the East River stood in between. Today, crossing the bridge on foot is a (sometimes daily) rite of summer passage. The view of New York Harbor is stunning and may cause you to stop and ponder as it did Walt Whitman. His poem "Crossing Brooklyn Ferry" (the bridge was built where the ferry used to operate) describes the city's enchanting, timeless rhythms.

Enter the bridge from Manhattan from Centre St., east of City Hall, nyc.gov

Crossing Brooklyn Ferry

It avails not, neither time or place—distance
avails not;
I am with you, you men and women of a
generation, or ever so many generations hence;
I project myself—also I return—I am with you,
and know how it is.
Just as you feel when you look on the river and
sky, so I felt;
Just as any of you is one of a living crowd, I was
one of a crowd;
Just as you are refresh'd by the gladness of the
river and the bright flow, I was refresh'd;
Just as you stand and lean on the rail, yet hurry
with the swift current, I stood, yet was hurried;
Just as you look on the numberless masts of
ships, and the thick-stem'd pipes of steamboats,
I look'd.

CATCH A PERFORMANCE
AT CARNEGIE HALL

"The amassing of wealth is one of the worse species of idolatry. No idol more debasing than the worship of money." Such are the words from a then 33-year-old Scottish immigrant who would become one of the world's richest men as well as the model for modern-day philanthropy. Andrew Carnegie's brick-and-mortar legacies are numerous in New York, but none has the enduring prominence as the music hall he personally financed in 1891. Situated at the corner of Seventh Avenue and 57th Street, the enormous building, which, ironically, doesn't have a steel infrastructure, presents upward of 250 concerts a year and can also be rented for private functions. All manner of performances have taken the stage, but orchestral music best showcases the concert hall's famed acoustics.

881 Seventh Ave., 212-247-7800, carnegiehall.com

VISIT THE 2ND FLOOR
GALLERIES OF CHELSEA

Yes, Chelsea has turned into a white box circus of commercialism . . . but so what? Millionaires need a place to buy art. For the rest of us, somewhat affordable art is just a staircase away, as many of the buildings in the gallery district have smaller, lesser-known spaces on upper floors. Granted, a lot of the art up there looks as if it were made by a group of fifth graders jacked up on Adderall, but maybe that's exactly what that big, bare wall in your living room needs.

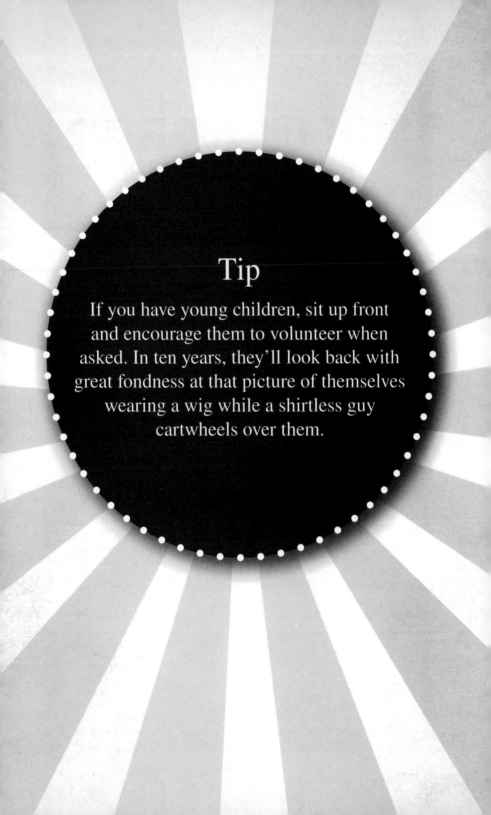

Tip

If you have young children, sit up front and encourage them to volunteer when asked. In ten years, they'll look back with great fondness at that picture of themselves wearing a wig while a shirtless guy cartwheels over them.

GIVE $20
TO STREET PERFORMERS

All over the city, particularly in the summertime, hundreds of New Yorkers supplement their income by entertaining passersby. Cellists and giant bubble makers may only deserve a couple of bucks, but organized dance and gymnastics groups go largely unappreciated, at least when it comes to compensation. The best acts are in Washington Square Park, where you can typically find a group of young men enacting a version of a routine being played out in other public spaces around the city. It lasts about 25 minutes and usually calls for embarrassing several members of the audience with racially charged jokes, interspersed with feats of strength and acrobatic daring. Before the grand finale, the men goad onlookers to fork over cash, but most people keep their hands in their pockets while looking askance at the ground. This is quality entertainment, people! So don't be a cheapskate.

nycgovparks.org/parks/washingtonsquarepark

ROCK OUT
AT THE BOWERY BALLROOM

Ever hear of the Go Team? How about Joan Baez or Soul Asylum? If not, then chances are you're not cool. Don't worry, though! A quick fix is only a gig away at this tiny concert venue, where bands from all over the world come to jam. The bar upstairs is a great place to amp up with friends before heading down to be electrified by music not meant for mass-market audiences. Obviously, you should do some homework and see a band that interests you, but any night rocking out at the Ballroom will be a night to remember. Quick, unrelated public service announcement: If you like John Mayer, pass on this suggestion—you're really too far gone.

6 Delancey St., 212-533-2111, boweryballroom.com

VISIT THE NATIONAL
SEPTEMBER 11 MEMORIAL & MUSEUM

Considering the unspeakable depravity that led to the creation of "ground zero," the feeling of reverence, endurance, perseverance, and peace that now greets visitors is truly astounding. More than 11 million people have come here from all over the world since it opened in 2011, and in so doing, advance the indomitable human spirit. The site is solemn, but it's also a place of wonder and learning, with the considerable effort of those who designed and built the memorial evident at every turn. The two massive reflecting pools that cascade water down into the footprints of the two felled towers are equal parts moving and beautiful. Bronze panels surrounding the pools bear the names of everyone who died in the attacks and are arranged with delicate significance. The museum, located seven stories underground at the base of the original Twin Towers, has created a powerful and extensive exhibit that includes crushed fire trucks, salvaged steel tridents that once supported the towers, photographs, and biographies of all those who perished in the attacks, including those of the terrorists, lest the world forgets who was responsible.

Liberty St., 212, 312-8800, 911memorial.org

WALK THE HIGH LINE

Considered this generation's Central Park, the 1.45 miles of reclaimed railroad track is testament to community activism and urban beautification efforts. Initially slated for demolition in 1999 until downtowners Joshua David and Robert Hammond started Friends of the High Line, the park now hosts more than 4.4 million visitors annually, which has actually become a problem. The path is only 30 feet wide in some places, causing a pleasant stroll to sometimes feel like waiting in line. So visit early in the morning or late in the evening, and avoid weekends at all cost.

The High Line runs from Gansevoort St. to W. 30th St., 212-500-6035, thehighline.org

Note

Developers may have lost the battle to tear down the High Line, but they won the war to build alongside it, as you will no doubt notice.

SEE A QUALITY
BROADWAY SHOW

Well, how original is this recommendation? It may seem obvious, but theater is one of those things that go largely unnoticed by anyone who isn't way into theater. And that's too bad. Because for every *Spider-Man Turn Off the Dark* financed by private equity groups, there's a musical, play, or one-man show produced by people for whom the Great White Way goes back generations. Don't you wish you could have seen Marlon Brando in *A Streetcar Named Desire* or John Malkovich in *Burn This*? While those performances are lost to history, you can still see their equal. Just pick up a copy of the *New York Times* and find out who and what is being hailed as the latest and greatest.

VISIT THE FRICK COLLECTION

What made the Gilded Age so, um, gilded? No income tax! Back in America's glory days before the U.S. government got all greedy, upstanding robber barons were allowed to spend their hard-earned money on what really mattered—like impossibly opulent mansions outfitted with entire rooms prefabricated in France. A number of these NYC masterpieces were tragically razed in the early part of the twentieth century, but the Frick mansion remains. It has a permanent collection that includes works by Monet and Renoir, but the real attraction is the house itself, which was built in 1912 by industrialist Henry Clay Frick to do his part entertaining the New York 400. (Google it.)

1 East 70th St., 212-547-6848, frick.org

GO TO THE NEW YORK PHILHARMONIC
ON NEW YEAR'S EVE

If you're more than 25 years old, then there's a good chance you no longer celebrate New Year's Eve in a bar. Luckily, the good people at Lincoln Center ring things in with a little more sophistication and a lot more noise—think Beethoven's Ninth Symphony, replete with endless bottles of champagne.

Avery Fisher Hall: 10 Lincoln Center Plaza, 212-875-5656, nyphil.org

PAY TRIBUTE
TO THE *INTREPID*

These 45,000 tons of steel now resting in the Hudson River went into action in 1943 and kicked ass around the globe until it was decommissioned in 1974. Highlights of the carrier's service include the battle during World War II off the coast of the Philippines when the ship took two direct kamikaze hits. In 1982, the aircraft carrier was given one final mission: to open as the Intrepid Air and Space Museum, thanks to the mighty efforts of real estate developer Zachary Fisher. Today, it features an SR 71 Blackbird, a Concord, a submarine, and even the space shuttle *Challenger* (sorry Houston!) on deck. But the main attractions are the salty dog volunteers who once served on the ship. They're more than happy to recount life at sea for anyone who's interested, and this group of heroes won't be around forever.

Pier 86:
W. 46th St. and Twelfth Ave., 212-245-0072, intrepidmuseum.org

DISAPPEAR
INSIDE THE MET

New York is lousy with esoteric museums—what, you've never heard of the Institute for the Study of the Ancient World on E. 84th Street? It's a different story, though, inside the baroque colossus that occupies the east frontage of Central Park between 82nd and 83rd streets. Its famed treasures are too numerous to list here, but with an operating budget of more than $250 million a year, it's the only museum in the world that rivals the Louvre in Paris. Properly exploring the museum in one day is impossible, but arrive early and consider the amazingly insightful audio tour.

1000 Fifth Ave., 212-535-7710, metmuseum.org

Don't Miss These Treasures

- *The Musicians* by Caravaggio
- *Autumn Rhythm* by Jackson Pollock
- Marble statue of the emperor Caracalla
- The dining room of Kirtlington Park
- The Egyptian room
- *The Harvesters* by Pieter Bruegel the Elder
- *Wheat Field with Cypresses* by Vincent van Gogh
- *Manuel Osorio Manrique de Zuñiga* by Goya

Tips

Never go on a weekend, and don't
pay extra to visit the 102nd floor
"Top Deck."

VISIT THE TOP
OF THE EMPIRE STATE BUILDING

It's a tourist trap for a reason. Built in 1931, this iconic landmark was the world's only true skyscraper for 40 years. A trip to the "Main Deck" on the 86th floor will cost you $27 and an hour of your life waiting in line, but once up there, the view in all directions is truly spectacular. Photo bugs should pay special attention to the northwest corner of the city, where a cluster of monochromatic tapered buildings makes for a neat shot.

350 Fifth Ave., 212-736-3100, esbnyc.com

JUDGE THE
SOLOMON R. GUGGENHEIM MUSEUM

Yes, another museum! But this one comes from the future, even though Frank Lloyd Wright, America's preeminent architect, designed it more than 50 years ago. The institution counts Kandinskys and Chagalls among its permanent collection and prides itself on extravagant and involved installations that often take over the soaring, swirling rotunda.

1071 Fifth Ave., 212-423-3500, guggenheim.org

Tips

The Guggenheim on Fifth Avenue
is part of Manhattan's Museum Mile.
Every June, for one day, Fifth Avenue
between 82nd and 105th streets is closed
to traffic, and pedestrians can visit ten of
the country's finest museums for free.
It's as good a time as any to check
this baby off your list.

DINE, DANCE, AND
LOOK UP AT GRAND CENTRAL STATION

This American landmark was almost a victim of the wrecking ball until one Jacqueline Kennedy Onassis lent her considerable support to save the train station and helped establish New York City's Landmarks Preservation Commission, which is charged with identifying and preserving culturally and architecturally significant buildings. (A public uproar ensued after the magnificent Penn Station was torn down to make room for the eyesore that is Madison Square Garden.)

89 E. 42nd St., grandcentralterminal.com

Here's What You Need to Know

1) The ceiling vault of the main room, elaborately decorated with the constellations of the zodiac, was restored to its former glory after a $175 million restoration in 1998. One of the white bricks was left covered in soot to remind people of how the building had fallen into disrepair . . . can you spot it?

2) Visit the Oyster Bar in the lower level, sit at the counter, and order a dozen oysters and a bowl of New England clam chowder.

3) Just outside the Oyster Bar is a vaulted ceiling where people standing in opposite corners can hear each other whisper.

4) Grand Central has one of the most beautiful bars in the city. It's called the Campbell Apartment. The 3,500-square-foot space was first leased in 1923 by John Campbell from William Kissam Vanderbilt II, whose family had built Grand Central Terminal.

5) There's a laser light show on the ceiling every hour on the hour during the holidays, and the main room turns into a ballroom on New Year's Eve.

6) Anderson Cooper's great, great, great grandfather, Cornelius Vanderbilt, built Grand Central in 1871 . . . just as an FYI.

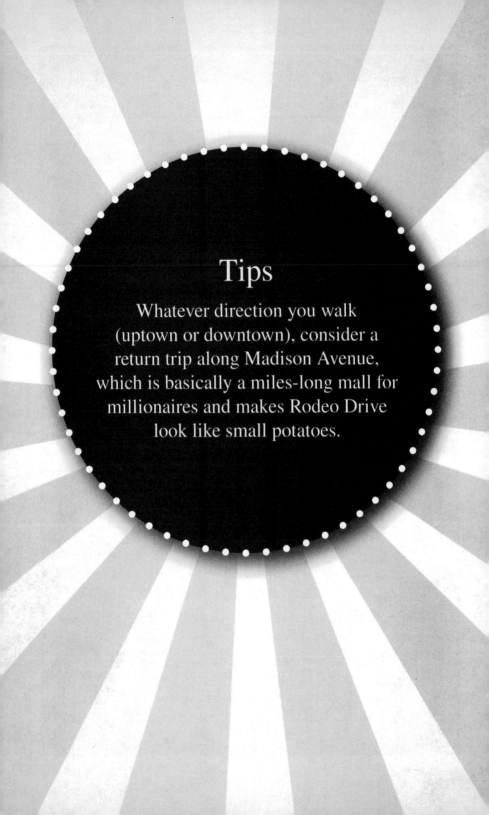

Tips

Whatever direction you walk (uptown or downtown), consider a return trip along Madison Avenue, which is basically a miles-long mall for millionaires and makes Rodeo Drive look like small potatoes.

STROLL ALONG
FIFTH AVENUE

Paris may have its Champs-Élysées and Barcelona its Las Ramblas, but no place struts its stuff better than Fifth Avenue between East 59th Street and East 110th Street. On one side, you have the idyllic beauty of Central Park; facing that man-made postcard is what amounts to a 51-block-long monument to America's unabashed wealth—soaring residential apartment buildings, gilded-age mansions, foreign consulates, world-class museums, private clubs—it's where the masters of the universe live and play.

BEHOLD
ROCKEFELLER CENTER

New York City takes and uses the best of what the world has to offer, and nowhere is that more apparent than in the heart of midtown, where an untold number of metric tons of glorious Indiana limestone occupies some 22 acres and rises 850 feet into the sky. Built during the Great Depression, the office complex was meant to symbolize humanity's progress toward new frontiers. Every day thousands of New Yorkers working at blue-chip companies (NBC, Time Inc., McGraw-Hill) headquartered there collide with tourists shopping at the Lego store, watching the *Today Show*, and heading to the observation deck atop the GE building. Winter is a special time of year for Rock Center, when the Christmas tree goes up and skaters of every skill level tear up the sunken ice rink. Often lost on locals and tourists alike is the extensive collection of artwork on the exterior and in the interior of every building. The *AIA Guide to New York* calls Rockefeller Center "the greatest urban complex of the 20th century."

rockefellercenter.com

Here's What's Not to Be Missed

- *Prometheus* by Paul Manship in the plaza

- *American Progress* by Jose Maria Sert

- *Atlas* sculpture by Lee Lawrie and Rene Paul Chambellan

- *Light and Movement* by Michio Ihara

- *Man at the Crossroads* by Diego Rivera

- Above all else, however, you must stand in the lobby of One Rockefeller Plaza at the top of any hour to truly experience its glorious beauty.

Tips

The easiest way to get to and from Yankee Stadium is via the No. 6 subway. If you arrive early, be sure to grab a pregame drink at one of the overcrowded sports bars on Jerome Avenue.

CATCH A YANKEES GAME

If you're not from New York—and even if you are—there's a good chance you're not a fan of baseball's greatest-ever team. Nevertheless, a trip to the house that Babe Ruth built should come before a trip to Cooperstown for any lover of America's National Pastime. Regular stadium seating tickets range from $100 all the way up to a ridiculous $200, though the $78 for the bleachers is a good option if you don't mind being cut off in the fifth inning (concession stands everywhere else serve until the seventh inning) and have a tolerance for vulgar chants and sporadic violence. Make sure you stay to the end to hear Frank Sinatra's "New York, New York," provided the home team wins!

1 E. 161st St., 718-293-4300, newyork.yankees.mlb.com

TAKE
THE 7 TRAIN

At the other end of the baseball spectrum are the Mets. There has been no good reason to ever see them play in recent years, but their new Citi Field stadium has made a name for itself among foodies. All the concession stands are managed by Danny Meyer of Union Square Cafe and Shake Shack fame, and during the game an equal number of fans can be seen watching the action on the field and standing in line for a burger or fish sandwich. Perhaps the best thing about heading out to Willis Point Station, though, is riding on the No. 7 train. Famously derided in 1999 by Atlanta's racially insensitive pitcher John Rocker, the train traverses the borough of Queens, which has the most diverse population in the United States. Each car is a little melting pot.

HAVE A BEER
AT McSORLEY'S

If you happened to see Martin Scorsese's *Gangs of New York*, then you know the lower part of Manhattan was once known as Five Points, denoting its five neighborhood districts. Today, no shred of those old gritty precincts remains, save for this bar that's been serving its own amber McSorley's Ale since the early 1900s. Unfortunately, McSorley's thirteen tables have become a destination for overgrown frat boys from New Jersey and Connecticut. Skip weekends and get there early to avoid the lines that invariably form outside. The suds come in 8.5-ounce glasses, so order a few at a time. And pace yourself, because once those glasses are empty, you'll be asked to either order another round . . . or get out.

15 E. 7th St., 212-473-9148, mcsorleysnewyork.com

GET A HAIRCUT
AT ASTOR PLACE

Need a trim but only have $16 and ten minutes? This one-of-a-kind mass-market barbershop near New York University's campus has been creating the latest street hairstyles since the 1940s. Walking into the place is akin to walking through a market in Marrakesh, as idle scissorshands looking for a customer will besiege you. Don't give into the pressure, and choose someone who gives you a good vibe. If you feel daring, ask them to give you a new look. You may not like your reflection at first, but you'll fit in nicely once you step outside.

2 Astor Pl., 212-475-9854, astorplacehairnyc.com

WATCH SOME NOIR
AT FILM FORUM

Several good independent movie theaters can be found in New York, but the Forum stands alone as cinema's obsessive historian. The atmosphere of the theater itself somehow matches the mood of the celluloid that lights up the big screen nightly. Foreign noir from Jean-Luc Godard and classics by Orson Welles are house specialties, but so are little-known gems like *Scarecrow* (starring Gene Hackman) and *Public Enemy* (which made Jimmy Cagney a star). So the next time you're wondering what to do on a Friday night, take a chance and catch a movie you've probably never heard of.

209 W. Houston St., 212-727-8110, filmforum.org

BUY A BOOK
AT THE STRAND

Here's a two-for-one special: Grab your old books, sell them at the Strand for a fair price, and then use the money to buy some new books! Opened in 1927 by Benjamin Bass, this downtown institution is famed for its "eight miles of books." New books are up front, and just about every other book in the English language is in the back and downstairs. Bring a cup of coffee—it's easy to get wonderfully lost browsing among all the sections and titles.

828 Broadway, 212-473-1452, strandbooks.com

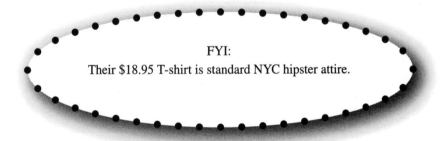

FYI:
Their $18.95 T-shirt is standard NYC hipster attire.

FIND A UNICORN
AT THE CLOISTERS

More money, more problems. No one can relate to that maxim better than John D. Rockefeller Jr., who had more than $100 billion (in today's money) burning a hole in his pocket during his lifetime (1874–1960). So to lessen that terrible burden, he set about giving it away. One of his most outrageous outlays of cash was for the Cloisters, a museum dedicated to medieval European art and architecture. Now a part of the Metropolitan Museum of Art, the museum was reconstructed from ancient monasteries, cloisters, and castles, imported brick by brick from Europe. Rockefeller purchased 67 acres of property in northern Manhattan as a site for the Cloisters as well as several hundred acres of the New Jersey Palisades across the Hudson River to preserve the view. The most significant part of the monastery-like building is the tenth-century Fuentiduña Apse, which was brought over from Spain, and is often used for concerts.

99 Margaret Corbin Dr., 212-923-3700, metmuseum.org

COOL OFF
AT LEMON ICE KING

Italian ice is a citywide summertime staple, and it's all more or less the same, but way out in Corona (off the LIE at exit 21, 108th St.) this storefront shop sells homemade frozen gold that's worth the trek. Bring napkins—they're not given out for some inexplicable reason—and if you go there at night, enjoy your ice while watching old-timers play bocce across the street.

52-02 108th St., 718-699-5133, thelemonicekingofcorona.com

Fun Fact:
This place is featured in the opening credits of the TV show
King of Queens.

WATCH NERDS
PLAY FOOTBALL

The tippity top of Manhattan plays host to one of the greatest embarrassments in all collegiate sports: Columbia University's football team. From 1983 to 1988, the Lions racked up a hilarious 0–44 record, making them a whipping post for the front pages of New York's newspapers. The team remains perennial losers—it's part of their charm, some argue—but the diminutive stadium, officially Robert K. Kraft Field, makes any game exciting to watch in an unusual setting, where the Harlem River meets the Hudson River. Only six games or so are played at home, so plan early and remember to keep expectations low.

gocolumbialions.com

HAVE A BLT
AT TOM'S RESTAURANT

It's where Jerry and the gang made a bet to abstain from masturbating, created a show about nothing, and fretted over crazy Joe Davola. It's not the actual diner where Seinfeld came up with his eponymous show's high concept with Larry David, but Tom's on the Upper West Side played the orange neon part in the sitcom. Truth be told, it's just like any other decent diner in the city, but slipping into one of its booths will take you back to the days when there was actually something good on TV on Thursday nights.

2880 Broadway, 212-864-6137, tomsrestaurant.net

WOLF A PIE
AT LOMBARDI'S

Depending on whom you ask and which neighborhood you're in, you'll get dozens of different answers as to who serves the best pizza in the city. Top contenders include Denino's in Staten Island, Louie and Ernie's in the Bronx, and Grimaldi's in Brooklyn. Actually, most pizza joints serve up equally delicious slices throughout the city, but there can be only one king, and that's Lombardi's Pizza in Nolita. Why? Because the Pizza Hall of Fame has recognized it as the first pizzeria in the United States (est. 1905), and the pizza has a one-of-a-kind taste. The place is constantly packed with locals, tourists, and loud Italian stereotypes from suburbia, so get there early and be prepared to wait, *capiche*?

32 Spring St., 212-941-7994, firstpizza.com

WATCH THE BALL DROP
IN TIMES SQUARE

How can you tell the difference between transplanted New Yorkers and born-and-breds? Ask them if they've ever gone to Times Square on New Year's Eve to watch the ball drop. Newbies will scoff at the idea, while just about everyone who's been raised in the city has made the pilgrimage at least once. To be sure, the experience is a complete horror show: You need to get there early (8 p.m. or so) for a good view of things, you shouldn't drink (there are no bathrooms), and you're standing shoulder to shoulder in the freezing cold with thousands of idiots like yourself. But once that countdown starts and the ball begins to drop, those little town blues will start melting away. Cascading confetti and a fireworks display complete the magical moment.

timessquarenyc.org

HAVE A DRINK
AT THE FOUR SEASONS

This restaurant, which opened in 1959, is famous for many reasons. It introduced the idea of seasonal menus. Artist Mark Rothko was commissioned to create three paintings but found the place so pretentious that he returned his advance. Regular lunch patrons are power brokers, like Caroline Kennedy, Ted Turner, and Henry Kissinger. The interior, which was designed by Philip Johnston, is the only interior in the city with New York Landmark status, and it is wonderfully unchanged from the day it opened. The four-sided bar is the best place to have a martini, just like all those Don Drapers used to do.

99 E. 52nd St., 212-754-9494, fourseasonsrestaurant.com

RIDE THE CYCLONE
AT CONEY ISLAND

The first train of cars began clinking up the wooden roller coaster in June 1927, and the thrill has never stopped. Along with the Wonder Wheel (also worth riding), the Cyclone has been the main attraction at Brooklyn's famed Coney Island Astroland (now called Luna Park). It began to decline in popularity after World War II and approached derelict status from the '70s to the early part of this century until a new stadium for the minor league Brooklyn Cyclones baseball team opened in 2001 right off the boardwalk and started to lure back families and hipsters. While the Cyclone is currently undergoing a five-year refurbishment in the off-season, it's still as creaky and scary as ever.

1000 Surf Avenue Brooklyn, 718-265-2100, lunaparknyc.com

Tip

Once the crossbar lowers across your lap, mention to your ride partner that three people have died riding the coaster.

HAVE SOME GLASS

New York City doesn't lack architectural marvels. From the Empire State Building to Rockefeller Center to the Chrysler Building, Manhattan's gridded canyons are like nothing else in the world. Two of the city's most influential gems, however, go largely unnoticed. Sitting catty-corner to each other on Park Avenue at 53rd Street are the buildings that ushered in the age of modern glass office towers: the Lever House and the Seagram Building. The Lever House went up first in 1952. Designed by Gordon Bunshaft and Natalie de Blois, it was the second skyscraper in New York whose outer walls are nonstructural (the first being the United Nations). The Seagram Building, completed in 1958, took innovation a step further. Designed by Ludwig Mies van der Rohe, the 38-floor monolith was the first building to incorporate the functionalism of its bronze-covered I-beams into the building's aesthetic appeal. Glass box buildings are so ubiquitous these days that the Lever House and Seagram Building may seem NBD, but picture them next to the brick-and-mortar building nearby and it's easy to see why they were both groundbreakers.

Lever House: 390 Park Ave.
Seagram Building: 375 Park Ave., 375parkavenue.com

LISTEN TO THE CARILLON
AT RIVERSIDE CHURCH

You used to be able to climb to the top of the 392-foot tower at this church to experience close-up the sonic boom of its 100 tons of bells, but like many joyful experiences in life, it was ruined by lawyers and their concern for "public safety." Still, every Sunday and on special holidays like Christmas and Easter, hand-directed recitals are played, and the best seats are the benches across the street in Riverside Park. The bells were a gift from John D. Rockefeller, and the main bell, the bourdon, is the largest carillon bell ever cast. There are 74 bronze bells in total, and during the day the bourdon marks the hours, and an automated drum plays Wagner's "Parsifal Quarters."

490 Riverside Dr., 212-870-6700, theriversidechurchny.org

GET MOONSTRUCK
IN BROOKLYN HEIGHTS

From any vantage point, Manhattan is a wonder to behold, but the best view is undoubtedly from the Brooklyn Heights promenade. Generations of New Yorkers have long cherished the walkway as one of the most romantic spots in the city, and films like *Moonstruck* and *Annie Hall* have made it a tourist destination in its own right. After getting your fill of Manhattan and the New York Harbor, explore the mansions that make up historic Brooklyn Heights, where in 1776 the English walloped General George Washington.

Tip

Pick up amazing takeout on Atlantic Avenue at Sahadi's, a Middle Eastern market, and eat it on the stoop of one of the neighborhood's many brownstones or on a bench on the promenade.

187 Atlantic Ave., Brooklyn, 718-624-4550, sahadis.com

EXPLORE PREHISTORIC
INWOOD HILL PARK

"According to legend, on this site of the principal Manhattan Indian village, Peter Minuit in 1626 purchased Manhattan island for trinkets and beads then worth about 60 gilders." So reads a plaque on the Shorakkopoch Rock, the supposed spot where the transaction took place in this 196-acre park at the northern tip of Manhattan that has remained *relatively* unchanged for thousands of years. Within the forest are salt marshes and caves as well as valleys and ridges made from shifting glaciers. Humans added paths, playgrounds, and BBQ areas, and, in 2002, bald eagles were reintroduced. It's the only non-landscaped park in the city, which is why exploring it is so much fun.

350 Dyckman St., nycgovparks.org

SEE SHAKESPEARE
IN THE PARK

As the Bard once said, "All the world's a stage, and all the men and women merely players." In this instance, you'll be playing the part of a joyful theatergoer while Hollywood A-listers attempt to do justice to iambic pentameter. For more than 50 years, these performances have been "the most beloved of the city's summer theater rites and a cherished New York institution," according to the *New York Times*. Tickets are free, given out in pairs to whoever shows up at the Delacorte Theater in Central Park the day of the performance. Top talent always headlines—alums include Al Pacino, Anne Hathaway, Liev Schreiber, Denzel Washington, and Martin Sheen—and there isn't a bad seat in the house.

shakespeareinthepark.org

Alexander Hamilton

Trinity Church: 74 Trinity Pl., 212-602-0800,
trinitywallstreet.org
Hamilton Grange National Memorial: 414 W. 141st St.,
646-548-2310, nps.gov/hagr

Ulysses S. Grant

The General Grant National Memorial:
W. 122nd St. & Riverside Dr., 212-666-1640,
nps.gov/gegr

Theodore Roosevelt

28 E. 20th St., 212-260-1616, nps.gov/thrb

PAY YOUR RESPECTS
TO AMERICA'S FATHERS

Aaron Burr mortally wounded Alexander Hamilton, one of America's Founding Fathers, in a duel on July 11, 1804, along the banks of the Hudson River. He is buried in Lower Manhattan in the graveyard at historic Trinity Church, which dates back to 1697. Before his death, Hamilton lived at The Grange, a house he had built in upper Manhattan. It was relocated to St. Nicholas Park at 141st Street and is now Hamilton Grange National Memorial, a museum celebrating the controversial statesman.

Ulysses S. Grant, the Civil War general and 18th president, completed his life's work on July 23, 1885. While many states squabbled about hosting his final resting place, New York City won out. The General Grant National Memorial (a.k.a. Grant's Tomb) is located in upper Manhattan in Riverside Park. It's a forlorn and moving place that leads you to contemplate America's tragic Civil War past.

The childhood home of Theodore Roosevelt, the only U.S. president to be born in New York City, is open to visitors Tuesday through Saturday, 9:00 a.m. to 5:00 p.m. The Rough Rider established our national parks, built the Panama Canal, and, as a trust buster, told John D. Rockefeller and J.P. Morgan to go to hell. And oh yeah, he also inspired the teddy bear.

SKATE
AT WOLLMAN'S RINK

The aesthetic contribution of any of Donald Trump's boxy buildings is open for debate, but in 1986 the real estate developer succeeded where the government failed when he took over the stalled renovations of Wollman's Rink in Central Park and got it operational, seemingly overnight. It first opened in 1949 and has since been the site of several movies and innumerable first dates. When there's snow on the ground and sun in the sky, skating in the park with skyscrapers as the backdrop is quintessential New York.

wollmanskatingrink.com

GET A TICKET
AT KATZ'S DELICATESSEN

Ever wonder what pastrami is, exactly? Well, it's actually beef brisket cured in brine and covered with a mix of spices that include garlic, paprika, and mustard seed. Then it's steamed until the meat begins to break down. The process was a way of preserving meat before the age of refrigeration. Today, there are only three quality delis that offer a traditional pastrami sandwich: Carnegie Deli, 2nd Avenue Deli, and Katz's Delicatessen. Each of these granddaddies has their share of history and old-time charm, but Katz's undoubtedly delivers the best experience. Upon entering, you're given a ticket (which you better not lose!), and then you proceed to the counter to order (your ticket will get marked depending on what you order). If you're a traditionalist, you'll want pastrami on rye with mustard and a cup of matzo ball soup. They'll throw in a mound of pickles for free. After taking that last delicious bite, take a stroll around the place to look at all the photos hanging on the wall and see if you can find the table where *that* scene from *When Harry Met Sally* was filmed.

205 E. Houston St., 212-254-2246, katzsdelicatessen.com

Tip

You don't have to enjoy diplomatic immunity to break bread with some of the most important people in the world. Anyone who makes a reservation can lunch at the Delegates Dining Room, which just underwent a three-year renovation. The menu changes daily and, not surprisingly, features cuisine from around the world.

RUB ELBOWS
AT THE UNITED NATIONS

It's one of the most famous places in the world but one of the least appreciated by the general public. The Secretariat Building, designed by Oscar Niemeyer and Le Corbusier, sits on an 18-acre site on the East River, which was donated by John D. Rockefeller Jr., and enjoys extra territorial status. Guided tours will bring you into the General Assembly and Security Council Chamber, point out treasures like a Norman Rockwell mosaic and Mark Chagall stained glass window, and, most important, provide the 411 on the organization's goals that range from abolishing the exploitation of children to promoting world peace.

760 United Nations Plaza, visit.un.org

SPEND AN AFTERNOON
AT THE RUSSIAN & TURKISH BATHS

Eastern Europeans may be as strong as oxen, but they sure know how to relax. Far from the très chic spas that populate Soho is this beloved sanctuary for the weary, indulgent, and hungover. A one-day admission costs $35, which allows you to enjoy the RTB's baths, steam rooms, and saunas (different days and times offer male-only, female-only, and coed mingling). Or you can pay extra for massages, Dead Sea salt scrubs, and the highly recommended Platza Oak Leaf beating, known affectionately as "Jewish acupuncture." Go with a friend and an open mind and you're guaranteed to leave walking on air.

268 E. 10th St., 212-674-9250, russianturkishbaths.com

SEE SELECTED SHORTS
AT SYMPHONY SPACE

If you're a fan of Selected Shorts on your local public radio station, then you owe it to yourself to see the real thing in person, but if you have no idea what Selected Shorts are, then listen up. Since 1985, sell-out crowds have been packing the Peter Sharp Theater at Symphony Space on the Upper West Side to see stage, screen, and television actors bring a select work of fiction to life. Guest authors and other literary figures typically cohost the shows, which are always smart, entertaining, and fun.

2537 Broadway, symphonyspace.org

GO SLEDDING
IN CENTRAL PARK

The problem with trying to go sledding in Manhattan is that there are precious few places to do it, and everyone descends on them the moment there is an inch of snow on the ground. Nowhere is the overcrowding more comical than at Pilgrim Hill on the east side of Central Park. On white weekends, it is packed with harried one-percenters trying to take photos of their Skylar and Edison flying through the sled traffic at terrific speeds. They regularly crash into other kids and parents walking back up the hill, so the mayhem is just as fun as the ride itself.

Enter the park at E. 72nd St. and Fifth Ave., centralparknyc.org

Tip

Some of the best hot chocolate in town
is a few blocks away at Via Quadronno.

25 E. 73rd St., 212-650-9880,
viaquadronno.com

HOLE UP
IN ARTURO'S

This simple Italian eatery has been around since 1957 and is the kind of place that, ideally, you should happen to stumble upon. The food is right out of grandma's kitchen—baked clams, linguine with mushroom sauce, veal cutlet Milanese—with the coal-oven pizza being the go-to menu item. The main draw, however, is the homey atmosphere and the nightly jazz quartet that plays in the front room. Another bonus is the generous, low-priced carafes of wine, which miraculously taste better as the night wears on. The leatherette booths are comfy, so go with friends and stay awhile.

106 W. Houston St., 212-677-3820

CHEER ON
THE ST. PATRICK'S DAY PARADE

There's no denying it: Practically every 20-something-year-old blockhead in the tri-state area descends on Manhattan every March 17 in their leprechaun finest and proceeds to get fall-down drunk. On the upside, bands, police, fire departments, and marchers come from all over the country and provide some six hours of bagpiping and high-stepping awesomeness. The first parade dates back to 1762—14 years before the Declaration of Independence—and now boasts upward of 200,000 marchers annually (automobiles and floats are not allowed). To complete the experience, have a pint of Guinness and some corned beef and cabbage at one of the many bars flying the Irish flag out front.

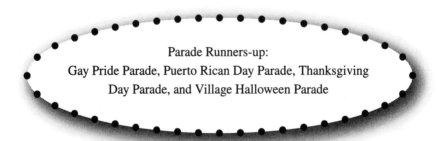

Parade Runners-up:
Gay Pride Parade, Puerto Rican Day Parade, Thanksgiving Day Parade, and Village Halloween Parade

RIDE A BIKE IN CENTRAL PARK
AT NIGHT

This must-do wouldn't have been possible 20 years ago, when entering the park after dusk was like being in a scene in *The Warriors*, but that was then, and this is now a wonderful experience that inspires therapeutic self-reflection (and fun and exercise). The park is closed to cars every day after 7 p.m., and you can choose any one of three different trails (1.7 miles, 5.2 miles, and 6.1 miles), all of which are illuminated by overhead street lamps, promising a fast-paced, cinematic adventure. What lurks in the shadows and beyond the next bend? That's exactly what you're there to find out.

Centralparknyc.org

LEARN SOMETHING
AT COOPER UNION

"Let us have faith that right makes might, and in that faith, let us, to the end, dare to do our duty as we understand it." So said Abraham Lincoln on the issue of slavery at this fabled institution of higher learning on February 27, 1860. The exalted speech helped him win the presidency and aptly demonstrated the enormous power of the spoken word. Cooper Union, which was founded in 1859 by inventor Peter Cooper and up until recently awarded full scholarships to every student, pays homage to that axiom with its lecture series that is as esteemed as it is eclectic. Speakers range from architects to politicians to folk singers, and the lectures don't cost a nickel to attend.

30 Cooper Sq., 212-353-4100, cooper.edu

WATCH THE SHOWDOWN
IN CHINATOWN

See if you can spot the pattern: Steve Nash, Thierry Henry, Grant Hill, Salomon Kalou, Tony Parker, Javier Zanetti—yep, NBA players and international soccer players. Every year since 2008, two-time NBA MVP Steve Nash has held his charity event, "Showdown," which pits two teams of eight ballers against each other for 40 minutes of play. It's held at a downtown urban field ("This is where we all started playing," Nash explains) and helps raise money for children's health. It's fun, it's free (you can pay for good seats and access to players), and it's for a good cause.

stevenash.org/showdown

VISIT
THE MORGAN LIBRARY & MUSEUM

Pierpont Morgan towered over Wall Street like no one before him or since. He helped establish America's modern banking system and helped finance the Industrial Revolution. He oversaw the creation of General Electric and U.S. Steel and was one of the wealthiest men in the world. By the time he died in Rome in 1913, Morgan had amassed an incredible treasure of written material, including medieval manuscripts, Thomas Cromwell's letters to King Henry VIII, sixteenth-century maps, and 1824 copyist scores of Beethoven's Ninth Symphony in his private library built adjacent to his New York residence. The library and museum underwent renovation and restoration in 2006 and have rotating exhibitions and concerts. The coolest part of admission, though, is getting to see Morgan's study and the resplendent library itself. FYI, you can leave your library card at home.

225 Madison Ave., 212-685-0008, themorgan.org

Tip

On your way out, take a look at the private dining room. Some 20 Japanese carpenters were flown in from Japan to construct the room in accordance with ancient techniques that forgo nails.

EAT WHERE THE SUN FIRST ROSE
IN NEW YORK

These days, there are as many sushi restaurants as there are pizzerias in New York. Of course, that wasn't always the case. In 1964, Nobuyoshi Kuraoka opened Nippon, formally introducing authentic Japanese cuisine to the city. The *New York Times*' food critic, Craig Claiborne, bestowed a three-star rating, and the rest is history. Good history too. Nippon was John F. Kennedy Jr.'s location of choice for his many first dates, and sister Caroline is still a regular. Yul Brynner ate at the restaurant every night after performing in *The King and I*, even ordering takeout from the hospital during his final days of battling cancer. The restaurant also introduced America to the sushi bar, which is where you should sit. The thing to order here is tempura "omakase" (chef's choice), which will be served piece by piece until you've had your fill.

155 E. 52nd St., 212-688-5941, restaurantnippon.com

CATCH A FIGHT
AT MSG

The self-proclaimed "World's Most Famous Arena" earned that moniker not because of a shockingly poor home basketball team or intermittent NHL championships but for showcasing boxing back in its glory days. In its Muhammad Ali and Howard Cosell days. In its "I coulda been a contender" days. If you stop to think about it, all of today's popular team sports are derivatives of this original mano y mano contest of strength, training, talent, and perseverance, which is why you need to see a slugfest up close and personal (most fights aren't held in the main arena). Tickets are cheap, and the seats are so good it's like being in the big palooka's corner.

4 Pennsylvania Pl., 212-465-6741, msg.com

Tip

If you just can't stomach a blood sport, a Knicks game, Rangers game, or concert in the main arena will punch this ticket.

RUN
THE NYC MARATHON

You know you want to, so the only question is whether you have the guts. Unlike other top marathons that require prior marathon experience, anyone 18 years or older with a heartbeat can enter the lottery to run (accredited runners are guaranteed entry). The first New York marathon took place in 1970 and was held in Central Park. It went citywide six years later, and now some 50,000 runners show up at the starting line at the Verrazano-Narrows Bridge in Staten Island to see all five boroughs the hard way. The record to beat, held by Kenyan Geoffrey Mutai, is 2:05:06. Good luck!

www.tcsnycmarathon.org

Alternative #1:
New York Road Runners Midnight Run in
Central Park on New Year's Eve
nyrr.org

Alternative #2:
The Five Boro Bike Tour held every May
bikenewyork.org

TUNE IN
AT BLEECKER BOB'S

Little by little, Greenwich Village, and indeed much of the city's bohemian downtown, is being transformed, block by grimy block, into downtown Houston. As in Houston, Texas. Tenement housing, oddball stores, and charming cafes are giving way to glass-box office buildings, European candle stores, and well-lit bank branches. Only a handful of '70s-era retail funk remains, one of the best being Bleecker Bob's. The record store sells every secondhand piece of vinyl worth collecting—from Bob Dylan to the Supremes to Led Zeppelin to new limited-edition albums.

118 W. 3rd St., 212-475-9677, bleecker-bobs.blogspot.com

PUT A QUARTER IN THE JUKEBOX
AT MANITOBA'S

Back in the good old '70s and '80s, the East Village used to be equal parts sex, drugs, and rock 'n' roll. Not anymore—the sacred punk music venue CBGB being defiled by a John Varvatos store marked the gentrification tipping point. One great dive remains, however, courtesy of Richard "Handsome Dick" Manitoba, lead singer of the NYC band The Dictators. The jukebox selection is a study in what music is supposed to be, and the Bob Gruen photos on the wall will make you ache for a world without boy bands.

99 Avenue B, 212, 982-2511, manitobas.com

THROW OFF YOUR BRA
AT HOGS & HEFFERS

Sometimes, you just gotta let loose—shot-drinking, dancing-on-the-bar, kissing-a-stranger kind of loose. In New York City, there's only one place built for such debauched revelry, and it's this biker bar in the Meatpacking District. The lone survivor of the neighborhood's transformation into an open-air mall by day and bridge 'n' tunnel mecca by night, this tiny watering hole made a name for itself when its clothing-challenged bartender, Michelle Dell, danced on the bar in an effort to stay warm. Her vivacious performance became the bar's trademark, and soon other female patrons joined in on the fun, and somewhere along the way undergarments started flying. To date, there are some 20,000 bras in the bar, one of which famously belongs to Julia Roberts. Of course, if you're not one to wear a bra, you can just take in the show.

859 Washington St., 212-929-0655, hogsandheifers.com

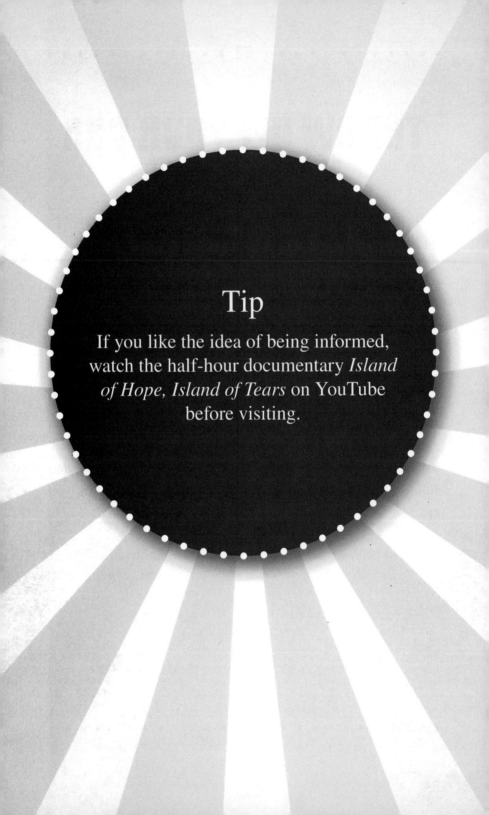

Tip

If you like the idea of being informed, watch the half-hour documentary *Island of Hope, Island of Tears* on YouTube before visiting.

REENTER THE U.S.
VIA ELLIS ISLAND

While the Statue of Liberty is better seen at a distance, America's primary port of entry during the first half of the twentieth century is best explored close-up. More than 17 million immigrants were processed on the island, and some 40 percent of Americans today can trace their family's heritage back to this spot. After Ellis Island closed in 1954, it began to fall into disrepair (along with the rest of the city). Then in 1982, President Ronald Reagan enlisted Chrysler honcho Lee Iacocca to spearhead private fund-raising efforts to restore both the island and the Statue of Liberty. The project eventually became the largest restoration effort in U.S. history. Visitors can tour the site's museum, use the Family Center to look up ancestors, peruse the 700,000 names inscribed into the Wall of Honor, or simply wander the island in quiet contemplation.

nps.gov/elis

MAKE A FRIEND
ATOP THE MET

From Memorial Day to Labor Day, New York is all about roof bars. They're in every Manhattan zip code and, for the most part, are identical in that each tries to out-cool the other. DJs! Pools! Apple martinis! The atmosphere ranges from interesting to insufferable, depending on how self-aware you are. But there's one watering hole in the sky that is truly oh-la-la. It's on the roof of the Metropolitan Museum of Art, and every summer a major installation is commissioned, so there's something new to toast up there. The views are absolutely stunning, but it's the concentration of interesting people—no Eurotrash or actuaries here—that will help make your visit memorable if you have the nerve to say hello. (An apple martini might help.)

1000 Fifth Ave., 212-535-7710, metmuseum.org

GO FISHING
AT LE BERNARDIN

What's the best restaurant in New York City? It's a question endlessly debated and one that seemingly has no answer. After all, "the best" is subjective, isn't it? No. Le Bernardin opened in France in 1972, moved to the Big Apple in 1986, and was immediately awarded four stars by the *New York Times*. Eric Ripert runs the kitchen now, and his tasting menu is what Neptune would want as his last meal. The service is as graceful and efficient as ballet, and the décor has the sexy drama of a Jean-Luc Godard film. It is the ultra nonplus for power lunches, but dinner is a treat of a lifetime.

155 W. 51st St., 212-554-1515, le-bernardin.com

SEE A SHOW
AT RADIO CITY MUSIC HALL

Like many other architectural wonders, this Art Deco entertainment temple almost went the way of the wrecking ball. First opened to the public in December 1932, the Music Hall now regularly hosts the NFL draft, the MTV Awards, Cirque du Soleil (if you're into that kind of thing), and all manner of rock, hip hop, and country music concerts. If you had to pick one, however, it should be the celebrated Christmas Spectacular, featuring the Rockettes. The tickets are pricey, and the lines are long, but the show never disappoints and can make a holiday impression on a child—and an adult—that can last a lifetime.

1260 Sixth Ave., 212-247-4777, radiocity.com

SEE A TAPED SHOW

Take your pick: *Saturday Night Live*, the *Late Show with David Letterman*, *The Daily Show with Jon Stewart*, *The Tonight Show Starring Jimmy Fallon*, *The Colbert Report*. Seeing a live taping in New York is an experience usually enjoyed only by the well connected, but anyone with a modicum of perseverance and patience can snag a ticket. The perennial hottest seat in town is SNL, which can be obtained by entering a lottery online (all the shows have lotteries) or by camping out the Friday before an airing to get a prized "stand by" ticket. Of course, there's no guarantee any of these shows will have on Angelina Jolie and not Carrot Top, but it's all about being a member of a live studio audience.

All ticket requests can be made online except for *Saturday Night Live*, for which you must wait in line. Check various shows' websites for details.

SPEND A NIGHT
AT THE HOTEL CHELSEA

Unfortunately, you're about 50 years too late to experience what Bob Dylan, Patti Smith, Allen Ginsberg, and others of the Beat Generation loved about this dingy National Landmark located on one of the most depressing streets in Manhattan. It was sold to a foreign developer and closed in 2011. That's the bad news. The good news is that the Chelsea will soon reopen, and while there is little doubt that the Interior of the '60s & '70s Past will have been professionally decorated out of existence, the façade and architectural bones of the hotel will remain. And so, too, might the infamous vibes that come from decades of unchecked alternative living and hedonism. Check in for the night . . . and then check out.

222 W. 23rd St., 646-918-8770, hotelchelsea.com

HAVE HIGH TEA
AT THE PLAZA

It's often the simple things in life that are most memorable. The English elevated afternoon tea to an art in the mid-nineteenth century when they colonized India and began importing its tea in large quantities. That legacy lives on in lavish splendor at the Palm Court in the Plaza, New York's most iconic hotel. Every day people from all over the world stroll into the dramatic domed atrium for a spot of tea (it comes with finger sandwiches and pastries) and some civilized conversation, which might touch on how the hotel is featured in F. Scott Fitzgerald's *The Great Gatsby* or how it's the home of the children's book character Eloise or how the Beatles stayed there on their first trip to the United States or maybe even how Charlie Sheen once trashed a room in a coke-fueled rampage.

768 Fifth Ave., 212-759-3000, theplazany.com

WATCH A STAR BEING BORN
AT THE APOLLO

Back in 1934, a nervous Ella Fitzgerald took the stage of the newly renamed Apollo Theater and sang two songs, "Judy" and "The Object of My Affection." It was Amateur Night, and the 15-year-old won first prize. A few generations later, Jimi Hendrix took home the same honors. The famous theater "where stars are born and legends are made" was at the center of the Harlem Renaissance during the decade leading up to World War II and helped kickstart the careers of superstars like Marvin Gaye, Diana Ross, Stevie Wonder, and Michael Jackson. The competition is held every Wednesday night, and members of the crowd, with their cheers and boos, help decide the fate of the night's performers.

253 W. 125th St., 212-531-5300, apollotheater.org

Tip

To hedge your bet and see
several quality acts, consider going on
a Super Top Dog night, when previous
Amateur Night winners battle for
a grand prize.

TOUR HISTORIC WALL STREET

Once upon a time, the intersection of Wall Street and Broad Street—the shared corner of the New York Stock Exchange and J.P. Morgan bank—was the financial capital of the world. Today, it's little more than a tourist destination. The mass exodus of investment firms and banks to places like Midtown and Jersey City began in the 1980s because executives wanted to be closer to Grand Central and Penn Station to shave time off their commute to suburbia, rents were cheaper elsewhere and, to be honest, the financial district has always been dreary and devoid of any meaningful retail or cultural activity. It was built early in the city's history and, as a result, the narrow streets and looming buildings practically blot out the sun. But more history is stuffed into the area than anywhere else in the city.

Financial District Highlights

The Federal Reserve Bank,
where the U.S. stores some $400 billion of gold.

33 Liberty St., 212-720-6130, newyorkfed.org

New York Stock Exchange,
the largest exchange in the world, doing more than $160 billion in transactions a day, is a National Historic Landmark.

11 Wall St., 212-656-3000, nyse.com

Federal Hall National Memorial,
where George Washington was inaugurated as the first president of the United States.

26 Wall St., 212-825-6990, nps.gov/feha

The Charging Bull sculpture,
designed by Arturo Di Modica, is the epitome of American success (and greed).

26 E. Broadway at Bowling Green Park

Canyon of Heroes,
where "ticker tape" has cascaded down on returning World War II leaders, Apollo astronauts, and championship sports teams.

Broadway, from Bowling Green to City Hall

Chelsea Market Highlights

Bar Suzette Crêperie

All crêpes used to be made equally, until the guys who run this place decided to fill their batter with things like French Onion Soup.

Beyond Sushi

Do you love the Japanese staple but worry about the world's supply of fish? Each one of these vegetarian sushi rolls is not only delicious but also a work of art.

Tuck Shop

This place specializes in Australian meat pies, but the sleeper dish here is kale salad. Hey, don't roll your eyes until you've tried it!

Friedman's Lunch

If it's service and comfort food you're after, Friedman's serves elevated diner fair and can make most anything on their menu gluten free.

Los Tacos No. 1

A food court isn't a food court without authentic tacos, and these are delicious enough to quiet any California food snob who claims no good Mexican grub exists on the East Coast.

Doughnuttery

The doughnuts are way overpriced, but damn are they tasty.

Buon Italia

Before you leave, stop by this grocery store to see what it's like to shop in Italy.

GO ON A FOODIE BINGE

Since the restaurant business is the second-largest industry in New York after the financial sector, it's literally—as in *literally*—impossible to taste, photograph, and post all the fabulous cuisine in the five boroughs. So here's a shortcut: eat your way through Chelsea Market. Built in a former National Biscuit Company factory (the Oreo cookie was invented there), the bottom floor serves as an international food court and shopping mall. Give yourself at least three hours, and choose from these highlights as your stomach allows.

75 Ninth Ave., 212-243-6005, chelseamarket.com

CAMP OUT
ON GOVERNORS ISLAND

Formerly a U.S. Army base and then a Coast Guard outpost, this 172-acre island—just a stone's throw—or short ferry ride—from lower Manhattan and Brooklyn is now a multi-use public space. A visit to the island on any of the 104 days it is open to the public is worthwhile: Bikes are available to tour the area, a beer garden serves fresh shellfish, there's a beach with a volleyball court, and rotating food and art festivals abound. And come 2015, an 80-foot-tall hill will be completed so that the able-bodied can take in the sweeping views of the city, the Statue of Liberty, and the Atlantic Ocean swelling just beyond the spectacular Verrazano-Narrows Bridge. Those aren't the reasons, though, why this Gov'ner is on the list. The reason is that one day a year the National Park Service, which runs the island, lifts its ban on camping, and all would-be adventurers are allowed to kayak, canoe, or boat to the island and spend the night in a tent. Support facilities are lacking, but such is the price that must be paid to fall asleep gazing at the stars and the tallest building in the Western Hemisphere.

govisland.com

SING KARAOKE
AT ARLENE'S GROCERY

You can't play a guitar like Jimi, and you can't sing like Freddie, yet you dream of being a rock star like Bowie, especially when you've been drinking. Sound familiar? Since 1996, this former bodega has been one of the primo showcases for local bands in NYC, and on Monday and Friday nights, their famous Karaoke band gives accountants, baristas, and repressed librarians a taste of the limelight. Even if you don't have it in you to take the stage, the drinks are cheap, and the people watching ranges from "wow" to "that's hilarious" to "what a train wreck." No matter the level of talent, though, the entertainment factor goes to 11.

95 Stanton St., 212-358-1633, arlenesgrocery.net

CONTEMPLATE
AT NUYORICAN POETS CAFÉ

Just once before I die
I want to climb up on a
tenement sky
to dream my lungs out till
I cry
Then scatter my ashes thru
The Lower East Side

Thus starts the epic "A Lower Eastside Poem" by Miguel Piñero, cofounder of Nuyorican, which began in a living room and has been called "the most integrated place on the planet" by Allen Ginsberg. Since its opening in 1973, the venue has been at the forefront of new literature, music, and theater. The programming is hypereclectic, so you might want to check out its website for calendar events, though Monday's open mic night is usually a risk worth taking.

236 E. 3rd St., 212-505-8183, nuyorican.org

BECOME A SCHOLAR

The reasons to visit the main branch of the public library on Fifth Avenue are numerous. For starters, the Beaux-Arts building itself is a historical jewel. Its initial patron was John Jacob Astor, whose fur trade business made him the first millionaire in America. His name, chiseled in white marble in the entryway, was the first of many to follow. At the north end on the first floor is the Periodicals Room, also known as the DeWitt Wallace Room, where the first issue of the *Reader's Digest* was cut and pasted together. In 2008, Stephen Schwarzman ponied up $100 million for a complete refurbishment of the building in exchange for his name being chiseled all over the place. The Rose Main Reading Room on the third floor is arguably the single most magnificent space in the city. Whatever you're searching for can be found for you and read here, but the library's most precious resource is the Rare Book Division. Anyone wishing to access its materials must register, but gaining permission is not difficult. Its collection includes material dating back to 1450 as well as the complete works of Voltaire in their original editions, the first four Folios of Shakespeare's works, a Gutenberg Bible, first editions of Goethe and Schiller . . . and Walt Whitman's personal copy of *Leaves of Grass*! Oh, by the way, it also has an original copy of the Declaration of Independence.

455 Fifth Ave., 917-275-6975, nypl.org

LIGHT A CANDLE
AT ST. PATRICK'S

Opened in May 1879, the neo-Gothic cathedral is a New York and National Historic Landmark. There's no reason to attend mass here, but lighting a candle will help pay for the cathedral's ongoing $180 million restoration (if not help bring about some minor miracle in your life). If you do want to attend mass, the most sought-after pew ticket is Easter, for which you have to request seats months in advance online. The service is televised, and the Easter Day Parade takes place directly outside afterward. Amen.

460 Madison Ave. (between E. 50th and E.51st), 212-753-2261, saintpatrickscathedral.org

Protestant Alternative

The Cathedral of St. John the Divine, located on Amsterdam Avenue at 110th Street in Manhattan's Morningside Heights neighborhood, is the largest Anglican church in the world. The liturgy is very progressive, and among its many special events is its annual New Year's Concert for Peace.

1047 Amsterdam Ave.,
212-316-7540,
stjohndivine.org

SHOP
UNION SQUARE GREENMARKET

Like most cities, New York has its share of farmers markets—places where farmers can sell directly to consumers. The city's first (modern) greenmarket began in 1976—the year of America's 200th birthday—and the outpost at Union Square is one of the first and definitely the best. Today, some 140 farmers, fishmongers, bakers, and florists descend on the park every Monday, Wednesday, Friday, and Saturday to sell their products the way they were meant to be bought. And buying some of everything should be your ultimate goal. Bring a big canvas bag, and stuff it with 100 percent grass-fed beef, a dozen free-range eggs, smoked farm trout, hydroponic herbs, heirloom vegetables, fresh-cut flowers, spicy pickles, lots of stinky cheese, wheatgrass juice, rooftop honey, and some freshly made gluten-free cookies for that high-maintenance friend of yours. And don't forget: Union Square is a park, so you'll want to pick up something fun for lunch and find yourself a bench. (Yes, wine is sold here too.)

Along E. 17th St., between Broadway and Park Ave. South, 212-788-7476, grownyc.org

DISCOVER WAVE HILL

If you could live anywhere in New York, where would it be? Some loft in Tribeca? A penthouse in Midtown? No, it'd be in the Bronx—in Riverdale, to be exact. That is where you'd find what is undoubtedly the most fabulous estate in the city. Established in 1843 by a lawyer, Wave Hill was expanded and enhanced by early conservationist and J.P. Morgan partner George Perkins. He rented one of the older buildings on the estate to distinguished individuals, including Theodore Roosevelt's family when the future president was a teenager and Mark Twain from 1901 to 1903. "I believe we have the noblest roaring blasts here I have ever known on land," Twain wrote of winter on the property. "They sing their hoarse song through the big tree-tops with a splendid energy that thrills me and stirs me and uplifts me and makes me want to live always." What really makes this place special, though, are the sweeping views of the Hudson River. Today, Wave Hill is a center for environmental studies, with a public garden and cultural center operated by the city, and offers classes ranging from gardening to woodworking to yoga. So while you may never be able to own the place, you can at least visit! (It's way cheaper.)

675 W. 252nd St., 718-549-3200, wavehill.org

VISIT
SAILORS' SNUG HARBOR

True story: A sea captain by the name of Robert Randall (1750–1801) deeded his 21 acres of land around and north of Washington Square to support a home for "aged, decrepit and worn out sailors" that became an 83-acre paradise on Staten Island for salty dogs in 1833. At one point, more than 1,000 sailors lived on the property, which features 26 Greek Revival Beaux Arts buildings and a grand music hall (the second oldest in New York after Carnegie Hall). With the advent of Social Security in the 1930s, the institution began to decline. In the '60s, a local coalition, with the help of the New York Landmarks Commission, saved the site from development, and in 1976, the Harbors Trustees moved the institution to the North Carolina coast. Today, the Snug Harbor Cultural Center and Botanical Garden is open to the public and offers a variety of classes, performances, and community service activities. A walk through the beautiful waterfront grounds, though, is as good a reason as any to visit. All thanks to the kindness of a stranger.

914 Richmond Terr., snug-harbor.org

HAVE LUNCH
AT BALTHAZAR

The crown jewel in celebrity restaurateur Keith McNally's empire is a sublime experience any time of the day, but no lunch place captures the joy and chic sophistication of the city like this Parisian-inspired eatery. The three-tiered, $155 Le Balthazar seafood platter is what you'll want to order to ensure maximum food envy from fellow patrons. Consider buying some pastries from the bakery next door before leaving, and don't forget to wave to Tom Cruise on your way out.

80 Spring St., 212-965-1414, balthazarny.com

EXPLORE
THE D&D BUILDING

Ever wonder how the superrich decorate their $35 million duplex penthouses and five-story townhouses? They hire an interior designer, who immediately heads to the Decoration & Design Building on Third Avenue in Midtown. For more than 45 years, it's been the showroom of choice for thousands of international manufacturers. We're talking entire kitchen systems from Italy, bathtubs chiseled from a single piece of granite, hand-carved teak wall units, $200,000 custom oriental rugs, made-to-order hammocks, and everything else millionaires need to keep up with the Joneses. Technically, common folk aren't supposed to visit the showrooms, but go ahead and do it anyway.

979 Third Ave., 212-759-5408, ddbuilding.com

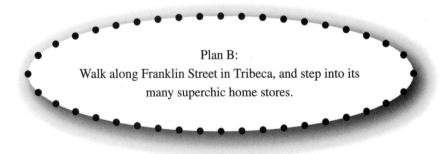

Plan B:
Walk along Franklin Street in Tribeca, and step into its many superchic home stores.

ATTEND
A WHITE BOX PARTY

Gallery openings are like complicated relationships—people who go tend to deride and adore them with equal passion, and alcohol is usually involved. Practically every opening serves inexpensive white wine—the fly tape needed to lure hangers-on, scenesters, and collectors alike—so it's best to drag along a friend to people watch with. Then there's the matter of deciding where to go. Midtown galleries sometimes attract people as one dimensional as a Burgoyne Diller painting, and while Soho still has its share of big-name galleries, Chelsea is the undisputed art mecca, with more than 75 galleries in a seven-block radius. What show should you attend? You have two options:

1. Find an exhibit of work that appeals to your aesthetic to ensure baseline entertainment (you can Google "Chelsea gallery openings" for current shows).

2. Go to any opening at one of the more prominent galleries, such as David Zwirner, Gagosian Gallery, The Pace Gallery, Paula Cooper Gallery, and Luhring Augustine, and behold the mwah-mwahing glitterati that show up.

3. There is, actually, a third option. Go to one of the tiny galleries in the Lower East Side or Chinatown. The upside is affordable art; the downside is no cheap white wine!

SCARF SOME PORK
AFTER MIDNIGHT

New Yorkers can burst onto the national scene in a variety of unexpected ways. They can, say, establish an epic baseball record (Babe Ruth, 1927), they can murder six strangers at the behest of their dog (David "Sun of Sam" Berkowitz, 1977), or they can reinvent the pork bun (David Chang, 2006). If you're a self-respecting foodie, then you've heard of the Korean-American chef who's built a nontraditional restaurant empire in the Lower East Side. Eating at any of his restaurants is a special occasion (his Michelin-starred Momofuku Ko is an impossible reservation), but heading to Momofuku Siam after midnight can ignite one of those special New York moments. Sit in the back room, where you can watch the mixologists creating all kinds of hocus-pocus drinks and order cocktails and pork buns one by one until you're satiated. Nothing more may become of the evening, but at least the next morning you'll wake up and mutter, "Damn, that was awesome!"

207 Second Ave., 212-254-3500, momofuku.com

SHOW UP
AT JOE'S PUB

The allure of walking down a dark alley is that you may discover something unexpected and exciting. The same can be said for going to Joe's Pub on any given night. The cozy venue at Astor Place features an idiosyncratic lineup of live acts from around the world, performing everything from jazz to rock to country to DJing to spoken-word events. Hundreds of top artists, including Norah Jones, Amy Winehouse, Pete Townshend, Henry Rollins, Prince, David Byrne, Mos Def, and Dolly Parton have taken the postage-stamp-sized stage, but the programming is so good that you'll enjoy whoever's billed. Opened in 1998, the nonprofit is named after Joseph Papp, the creative force behind the nearby Public Theater and Shakespeare in the Park. The pub is intimate, dimly lit, boasts superb acoustics, and always serves stiff drinks—so there's nothing to be afraid of.

425 Lafayette St., 212-539-8778, joespub.com

Tips for
Buying Art

- Take photos of the areas in your home that need art so that you can refer to them when you want to visualize a work in a certain space.

- Ask questions. Galleriests are there to educate you about their wares, so bend their ear.

- Walk around the entire fair before seriously deciding whether or not to buy something.

- Bring a friend whose taste in art you trust. Even though art should be a gut buy, there's nothing wrong with some friendly advice.

- Remember that you get what you pay for.

BROWSE
THE AFFORDABLE ART FAIR

Back in 1996, Will Ramsay knew his fellow Englishmen had a problem. Namely, they wanted to buy art but didn't know how to find anything within their budget. So he opened Will's Art Warehouse, with the idea of selling quality art in a no-pressure environment at reasonable prices. Some 10,000 people flocked to the Warehouse, so Will decided to take his concept on the road. Today, his Affordable Art Fair is held in cities around the world, and New York's kicks off every April and lasts four days. More than 75 galleries participate, and prices for the art ranges from $100 to $10,000. All manner of paintings, sketches, prints, lithographs, sculptures, and mediums are for sale, so you have a good chance of finding something just right.

269 Eleventh Ave., 212-255-2003, affordableartfair.com

TAKE
A COOKING CLASS

There are three kinds of people in this world: those who can't cook, those who think they can cook, and those who know how to make a roux, béchamel, or chocolate soufflé from memory. And while cookbooks can help any kitchen jockey prepare a meal, there is no substitute for personal instruction from a master chef. Want to learn how to make pizza? There's a school for that (Pizza a Casa Pizza School). Want to cook like they did back in *Little House on the Prairie* days? There's a school for that (Natural Gourmet Institute), but if you want an all-around, intermediate-level education, consider one of these three options:

Institute of Culinary Education

Chefs like Mario Batali and Daniel Boulud hire graduates from this school that churns out thousands of professionals a year. Their kitchens are tops, as are their varied recreational classes.

50 W. 23rd St., 212-847-0700, ice.edu

International Culinary Center

This school lets you learn French cooking techniques à la carte. One-day classes range from French classics to eclairs to croissants to baguettes.

462 Broadway, 888-324-2433,
internationalculinarycenter.com

The New School

New York's alternative university offers a wide range of courses that follow trends like molecular gastronomy, farm-to-table meals, and preparing meals from cooking shows. The classes are not only fun but also affordable.

66 W. 12th St., 212-229-8900, newschool.edu

TAKE A CHILD
TO FAO SCHWARTZ

The origins of this toy store date back to the Civil War, which is appropriate since a trip to FAO Schwartz is like heading into battle. The place is always jam-packed, and it's impossible to escape without spending a small fortune, but, hey, children love it. The floor piano made famous in *Big*, the movie starring Tom Hanks, should be your first stop. Have your smart phone at the ready because adorable moments come fast and furious. After your kids' toes have been twinkled out, it'll be time to explore. The enormous two-story store, with its giant stuffed animals, character action heroes, and elaborate displays, creates nothing short of a wonderland that makes finding the perfect toy just as much fun as playing with it. Helicopters, rare Lego sets, life-sized teddy bears, custom-made Muppet dolls, handmade dollhouses, karaoke systems—there's something to satisfy even the most spoiled child.

767 Fifth Ave., 212-644-9400, fao.com

DON'T FUHGEDDABOUD
ARTHUR AVENUE!

The neighborhood business association bills itself as "The real Little Italy of New York," which is only half true. Like most neighborhoods that once had a strong, proud European ethnic identity, Arthur Avenue ain't what it used to be. Located in the Fordham section of the Bronx, this pocket of Italian restaurants, markets, and cafes caters to the neighborhood's first- and second-generation holdouts from the old country and yuppies who make the pilgrimage for a night of tomato sauce and chianti. The thing to keep in mind is that the food can be very good but not great. While that may not sound like a ringing endorsement, the overall experience is very satisfying. Two safe bets are Dominick's and Pasquale's Rigoletto. For dessert, forgo offerings at the restaurant, and walk along the avenue until you see a pastry shop calling your name.

arthuravenuebronx.com

Plan B:
One Sunday every September Arthur Avenue hosts its Ferragosto street fair, celebrating the end of the harvest season. It runs from 11 a.m. to 7 p.m. and features yummy Italian food, live music, and kids activities.

ATTEND AN AUCTION
AT CHRISTIE'S

Every year or so the auction house in Rockefeller Center assembles a blockbuster that touts the most sought-after names in the world: Jackson Pollock, Edgar Degas, Pablo Picasso, Andy Warhol, Mark Rothko, Willem de Kooning, etc. The auction typically lasts two hours, and by the time the gavel strikes the final "sold," more than $400 million will have changed hands. These auctions are standing room only, so requesting a ticket early is a must. (Christie's coveted mega collectors sit in skyboxes on the second floor.) For more than a week before the auction, you can visit Christie's during the day and admire all the work up close and personal. There's hardly anyone ever there, so it's like walking through a small, peaceful museum of masterpieces.

1230 Sixth Ave., 212-636-2000, christies.com

BECOME AN EXTRA
AT BEMELMANS BAR

If you're looking for some escapism, head to this celebrated mainstay in the Carlyle Hotel on the Upper East Side, which is the closest gin joint New York has to Rick's Café Americain. It's named after Ludwig Bemelman, author of the Madeline children's books, who painted the whimsical wall murals depicting French school children and ice-skating rabbits that define the space. Adding to the charm are dimly lit tables, chocolate-brown leather banquettes, and a ceiling covered in 24-karat gold leaf. These old-world touches contribute to an atmosphere that is both romantic and cinematic, in which every patron is a participating character actor. In the middle of the small space is a piano that comes alive every evening, as the crowd of beautiful people and megawatt celebrities (fans include Ron Wood, Jack Nicholson, and Leonardo Di Caprio) order one of the bar's famed cocktails. So dress appropriately—people are watching!

35 E. 76th St., 212-744-1600, rosewoodhotels.com

EXPLORE
THE BRONX ZOO AND NEW YORK BOTANICAL GARDEN

These two destinations should, ideally, be separate entries, but they both occupy the same park area in the Bronx and can easily be surveyed in one day, providing you're wearing sensible shoes. The Botanical Garden was the first to open in 1891, with the Zoo roaring to life only eight years later. Highlights at the Garden include its Italian Renaissance greenhouse, the Rose Garden, and the 50-acre old-growth forest. Over at the Zoo, you've got Tiger Mountain, camel rides, Congo gorillas, and a monorail that takes you on a tour of Asia in minutes! Of course, the Zoo and Garden are much more than day-tripping destinations: They're academic institutions that offer lecture series, host special events, and support research in their respective fields. So if you want more after your first visit, become a member at either place and create a to-do list all your own.

2300 Southern Blvd., Bronx, 718-367-1010, bronxzoo.com & nybg.org

Bonus Points

If you have the energy and
want to go for the trifecta, a few blocks
west of the Botanical Garden is the Poe
Cottage, where Edgar Allan Poe lived
out the last few years of his life.

2640 Grand Concourse,
718-881-8900, bronxhistoricalsociety.org

HIT THE LINKS
AT DYKER BEACH GOLF COURSE

It's funny how perceived value can affect the prices of things. Take golf, for instance. On the Jersey side of the Hudson River sits Liberty National Golf Course, which cost $250 million to build, counts Rudolph Giuliani and Eli Manning among its members, charges $250,000 to join, and has views of the Statue of Liberty. Getting to the course from the financial district takes mere minutes, if you go by helicopter. (Yes, they have an on-site helipad.) Across the East River in Brooklyn, however, a golf course of a lesser god resides. Dyker isn't as snazzy as Liberty, but it is easy to get to from lower Manhattan via the 6 train or taxi. The par 72 course also boasts views of the Verrazano-Narrows Bridge, immaculate greens, a wonderful bar and grill, and, best of all, it's open to the public. Anyone can reserve a tee time online, and prices range from $19.25 for early birds looking to shoot 9 holes to just $49 for 18 holes on weekends.

1030 86th St., 718-836-9722, dykerbeachgc.com

WATCH SOME FOOTIE
IN QUEENS

There's been an explosion of beer halls in Manhattan and Brooklyn in recent years, attracting the usual loud, thirsty rabble—hipsters, office drones, bachelorettes, frat boys. At the other end of the spectrum stands the Bohemian Hall & Beer Garden in Astoria, Queens. Established in 1910, it's New York's oldest beer garden, and it definitely shows. Enclosed by a looming brick wall, the massive space could be mistaken for a parking lot if not for the mass-market wooden benches and two stages. When full of revelers and live music, however, it's a thing of beauty. Bohemian started as a Czech social club, and so the menu features standbys like potato pancakes and klobasa to be washed down with mugs of Krusovice and Staropramen. Any day in the summer is a good time to go (the bar is opened year-round), but if you're a soccer fan, go during the European Cup or World Cup. Projection screens are set up, and the borough's ethnic fans come to cheer, drink, and celebrate with their fellow New Yorkers.

29-19 24th Ave., 718-274-4925, bohemianhall.com

BINGE
ON PERFORMANCE ART

If a tree falls in a forest, does it make a sound? Yes. If a naked Japanese gentleman dances to electronic house music while throwing paint at teddy bears, is it performance art? Also yes, but only if there's someone there watching. Galleries and the city museums have always offered their share of live installations, but in 2005, performance art got organized, commercialized, and served up for the masses. That's when performance art pioneer and historian RoseLee Goldberg unveiled Performa, a three-week lineup of multidisciplinary events held all over the city. The biennial kicks off with a gala, and more than 100 international artists participate. Shows range from films to concerts to stage productions to audience participation stunts to bizarre one-person shows. The trick to getting the most out of Performa is to go to as many events as possible, which allows you to not only compare the merits of each show but also to acquire an appreciation for hard work and talent involved . . . even if it's not your thing.

performa-arts.org

BREAK YOUR BACK
AT THE GIGLIO FEAST

Ask any New Yorker to sum up Williamsburg, and chances are they'll tell you it's ground zero for cooler-than-thou Brooklynites. Actually, the neighborhood has been way cool since 1903, when immigrants from southern Italy decided to import the tradition of celebrating Saint Paulinus. Unlike the more famous San Gennaro festival held in Manhattan, the Giglio Feast distinguishes itself by the elaborate, superheavy floats that dozens of men—young and old—carry down Havemeyer Street on their shoulders. The largest is an 80-foot-tall steeple-like structure, which sits atop a base that also holds a brass band belting out old-timey marching music, much to the delight of the surging crowds and sweaty beasts of burden underfoot. The feast, which sizzles with all kinds of Italian street food, is run by Our Lady of Mount Carmel Church and is held in the hottest month of the year, July. How's that for Catholic guilt?

olmcfeast.com

KAYAK THE HUDSON

Every summer volunteers at the nonprofit Downtown Boathouse help thousands of New Yorkers get up close and personal with the majestic Hudson River. And while kayaking in a mega metropolis may seem a bit odd, it's actually a wonderful outdoor experience, made even more so because it's free. There are three Boathouse locations—Pier 40, Pier 96, and at 72nd Street—that offer kayaks, paddles, and life jackets on a first-come, first-served basis. Pier 40 and Pier 96 even have lockers and a rinse-off station, not that there's any need to worry about the cleanliness of the water—General Electric stopped dumping PCPs into the river back in 1977!

hudsonriverpark.org

BRING A WAD OF CASH
TO PETER LUGER

"The best meal of my life was at Peter Luger." That was Johnny Carson talking about the porterhouse he ate at this New York institution that's been around since 1887. But don't take his word for it. Zagat has rated it the No. 1 steak house for 30 years in a row. The waiters are notoriously gruff, the restaurant doesn't take credit cards, and the ambiance is a slight step up from a beer hall, but unless you eat their dry-aged beef at least once, you'll have misspent your time on earth.

178 Broadway, Brooklyn, 718-387-7400, peterluger.com

FIND HAPPINESS
IN CHINATOWN

If there's one neighborhood in Manhattan that's worthy of a full day of exploration, it's this frenetic district in lower Manhattan. Immigration reform in the '60s led to an influx of Chinese, who settled in the tenement apartments neighboring Little Italy, eventually enveloping it. The two main commercial thoroughfares are Mott Street and East Broadway, where merchants sell everything from exotic fruits to fresh fish, cheap trinkets to gold jewelry, Peking duck to live eels and frogs. The number of shops and restaurants are seemingly endless, and deciding where to eat is part of the adventure. If all that walking begins to test your stamina, consider getting a foot or body rub in one of the area's countless budget massage parlors—contrary to popular belief, they're all legit and really good!

DISCOVER BROOKLYN

Although a few entries from this fabled borough are on this list, Brooklyn itself deserves special mention. Over the course of the past 20 years, Brooklyn has been transformed from the less-expensive alternative to Manhattan into a breakout cultural superstar heard around the world. The Brooklyn Academy of Music (BAM), Fort Greene, Brighton Beach, Prospect Park, the Barclays Center, DUMBO, the Brooklyn Flea, Flatbush, Jane's Carousel on the new waterfront—these are only a few of the attractions that have made Brooklyn a global brand. Three-star and cutting-edge lesser-known restaurants, cafes, markets, and shops abound, but it's also the rejuvenated old-world neighborhoods and never-say-die bakeries, butchers, and ethnic food stores that cultivate the irresistible charm. Park Slope is a good starting point for novice explorers; the more daring can hop on the L train in Manhattan and hop off wherever their little heart desires.

SUGGESTED ITINERARIES

THE PERFECT DAY IN CITY

LONG WEEKEND OPTIONS

HITS FOR MUSIC LOVERS

• •

• •

THE GREAT OUTDOORS

FOODIE FAVORITES

OUTER BOROUGH EXPERIENCES

• •

FUN WITH KIDS

• •

ACTIVITIES
BY SEASON

SUMMER

FALL

• •

INDEX

• •

• •

• •

• •